SMELLING THEIR PREY
ANIMALS WITH AN AMAZING SENSE OF SMELL

written by Kathryn Lay
illustrated by Christina Wald

magic wagon

visit us at www.abdopublishing.com

Published by Magic Wagon, a division of the ABDO Group, PO Box 398166, Minneapolis, MN 55439.
Copyright © 2013 by Abdo Consulting Group, Inc. International copyrights reserved in all countries. All rights
reserved. No part of this book may be reproduced in any form without written permission from the publisher.

Looking Glass Library™ is a trademark and logo of Magic Wagon.

Printed in the United States of America, North Mankato, Minnesota.
052012
092012
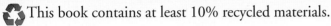This book contains at least 10% recycled materials.

Written by Kathryn Lay
Illustrated by Christina Wald
Edited by Stephanie Hedlund and Rochelle Baltzer
Cover and interior layout and design by Neil Klinepier

Library of Congress Cataloging-in-Publication Data

Lay, Kathryn.
  Smelling their prey : animals with an amazing sense of smell / written by Kathryn Lay ; illustrated by Christina
Wald.
      p. cm. -- (Sensing their prey)
  Includes index.
  ISBN 978-1-61641-868-7
  1. Smell--Juvenile literature. 2. Senses and sensation--Juvenile literature. 3. Animal behavior--Juvenile literature.
I. Wald, Christina, ill. II. Title.
  QP458.L39 2013
  573.8'77--dc23
                                    2011052277

CONTENTS

Is That Dinner I Smell?

Animals must find their own food every day. A good sense of smell is necessary for many animals to find food. They might have poor hearing or eyesight, but their sense of smell is strong. Many carnivores track their prey by smell. Even some herbivores use this sense to find plants to eat.

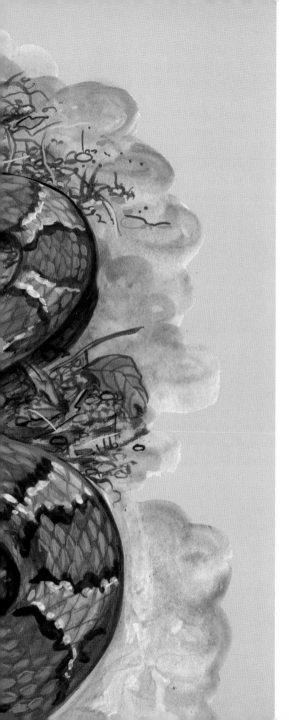

A Smelling Tongue

A snake uses its tongue to smell. You might see a snake flicking its tongue in and out. It is smelling the air by picking up dust particles. These particles are carried to taste detectors in the snake's mouth.

Flick your tongue in the air. Can you smell your dinner without your nose?

A special organ in the roof of the snake's mouth sharpens its sense of smell. This is called the Jacobson's organ. The scent's chemicals are taken by the tongue to the Jacobson's organ. It lets the snake know what animals are near.

Human tongues are for tasting only, so you'll have to smell food with your nose.

Brain

Jacobson's organ

Tongue retracted
with scent to organ

Smelling Down Under

Some animals can smell prey that is underground. Foxes are able to smell food that is buried under two feet (.6 m) of soil!

The wild pig has a strong sense of smell. When it smells tubers, it digs with its large nose to find its food.

A Long, Long Nose

The giant anteater eats mainly ground-dwelling ants. It sometimes eats termites and army ants, which live underground. The anteater's strong sense of smell finds the ants from the top of the ground. Then, it slurps them up with its long tongue!

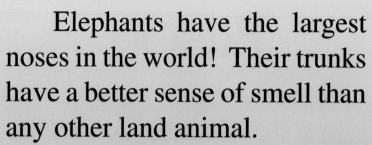

Elephants have the largest noses in the world! Their trunks have a better sense of smell than any other land animal.

An elephant is constantly moving the tip of its trunk to smell. Sometimes, it touches its trunk on something. Then, it uses the Jacobson's organ in its mouth to find out what the smell is—just like a snake! This is called the flehmen response.

The Smell of Blood

A shark is able to identify different smells found in the ocean. Water flows in and out of the nostrils. They use the scents to decide which ones are food.

A shark can recognize one drop of blood in 1,000,000 parts of water. Sharks react strongly to the smell of fresh blood in the water. An injured shark will even try to eat itself!

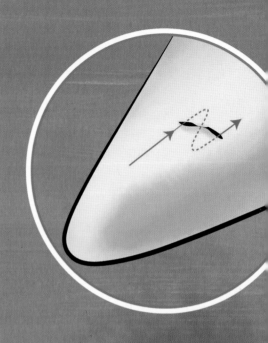

Predators such as lions and hyenas can smell blood from far away, too. They choose whether it is something they want to eat or ignore.

How far away can you smell food? Does it have to be in the same room? How about in the same house?

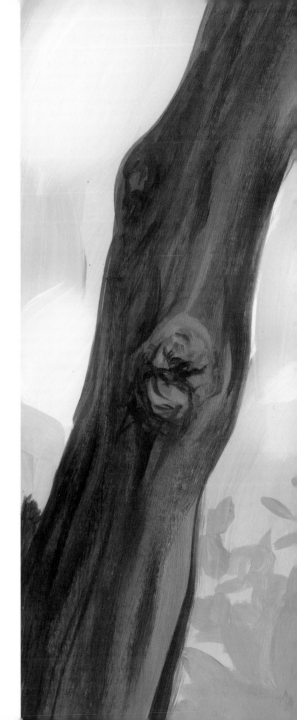

I Know That Smell!

Most dogs are able to follow their prey before they even see it. A coonhound knows when a raccoon's track was made, how fast it was traveling, and in what direction. It ignores the scent of any other animal except the one it is chasing.

If one friend was on the other side of the cafeteria with a hot dog and another friend was on a different side with a plate of spaghetti, could you figure out which was which by only sniffing?

THAT FRUIT
SMELLS GREAT

Fruit bats find their way by using echolocation and sight. But, they locate ripening fruit, such as mangoes, by smell. That way, they can fly right to the food they enjoy.

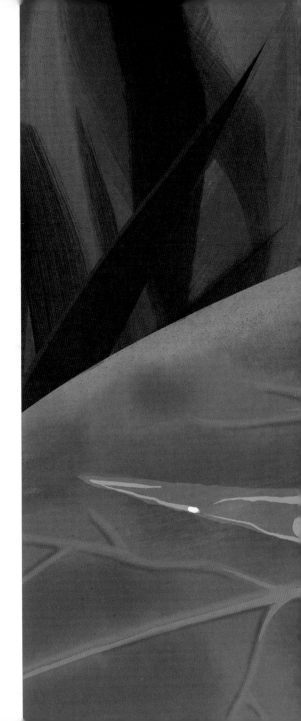

Don't Need a Nose to Smell

Snails also use their sense of smell to find food. Their diet includes vegetables, fruits, and decaying plants. They even eat dirt if there is nothing else. They use their antennae to recognize chemicals given off by plants.

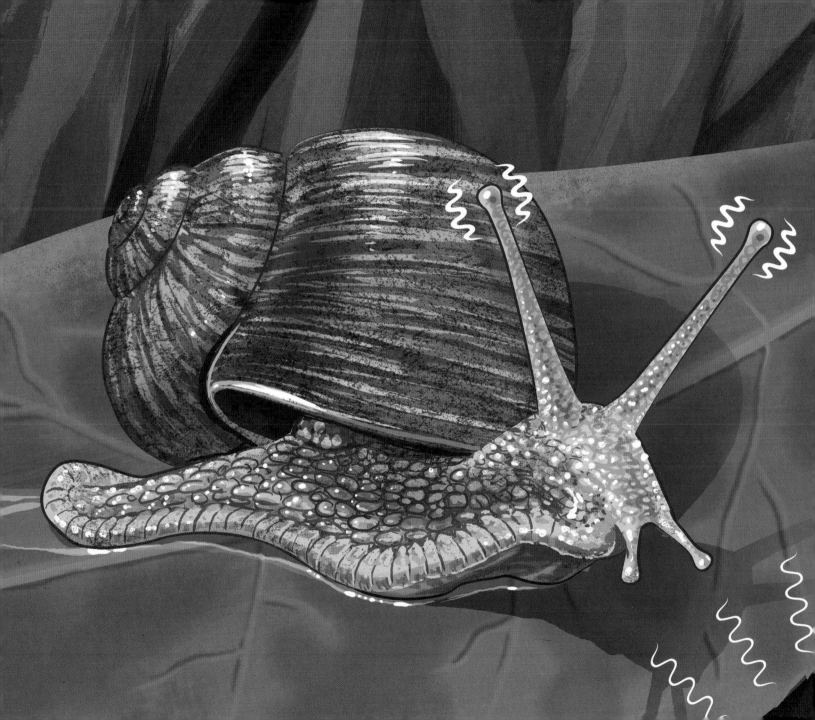

LEARNING ALL ABOUT DINNER

Smell is very important to a wolf. If an animal is downwind, a wolf can track its scent. A wolf can smell its prey from nearly two miles (3 km) away.

A wolf's sense of smell is strong enough to tell the difference between its pack, enemies, and prey. Once it has the scent of prey, it moves ahead of it to make the kill.

A bear's sense of smell is 2,100 times better than a human's! Bears can smell a dead animal that is upwind and as far away as 20 miles (32 km).

The area of the brain that directs the sense of smell is called the olfactory bulb. A bear's olfactory bulb is five times bigger than a human's. Its nose has hundreds of tiny muscles that move it as easy as people move their fingers.

Without their amazing sense of smell, many animals would go hungry. Can you smell food cooking at home or school? It must be time to eat!

Glossary

antennae (an-TEH-nee) - a pair of thin sense organs connected to the top of an insect's head.

carnivore - an animal or a plant that eats meat.

decaying - breaking down into simpler parts.

downwind - in the direction the wind is blowing.

echolocation - a process for locating distant or unseen objects by using sound waves.

herbivore - an animal that eats plants only.

organ - a part of an animal or a plant that is made of several kinds of tissues and does a certain job.

particle - the smallest amount of something.

tuber - an underground stem that has a bud and may produce a plant.

upwind - into the wind.

Index

Web Sites

To learn more about animal senses, visit ABDO Group online at **www.abdopublishing.com**. Web sites about animal senses are featured on our Book Links page. These links are routinely monitored and updated to provide the most current information available.

WITHDRAWN